ideals® CHRISTMAS

The ringing of the church bells;
the moonlight on the snow;
children dressed like Eskimos,
caroling as they go;
stockings by the fireplace;
the wreath upon the door—
they tell us Christmastime is here,
with all its joys, once more.

—Jean E. Koch

ideals®
NASHVILLE, TENNESSEE

At Christmastime

Elisabeth W. Winstead

Sing a song of Christmas,
of streamers, green and red,
of windy, icy weather
just right for skate and sled.

Sing a song of Christmas,
of candlelights aglow,
of cookies and plum puddings,
of freshly fallen snow.

Sing a song of Christmas
as shoppers homeward go,

of cheery yule log blazing,
of stockings in a row.

Sing a song of Christmas,
star-sprinkled sky above;
Christmas bells are ringing out
sweet songs of peace and love.

Sing a song of Christmas;
may laughter, love, and cheer
possess our hearts on Christmas Day
and through a bright new year.

Christmas Is Coming

Solveig Paulson Russell

Oh, hide the gifts and stir the cakes,
for Christmastime is coming;
about the house the youngsters prance
and Mother's work is humming.

Our home is bright with streamer things
and presents in the making,
and all the air is tingling with
the spicy things a-baking.

Oh, feed the flame and chop the wood,
and bring in greens and trimming . . .
with Christmas mirth and happiness
the whole house is a-brimming!

There's sparkle in each merry eye,
and lips are set for funning,
and every heart's a-tune with joy—
for Christmas is a-coming!

**The Master Painter dipped His brush
in diamonds sparkling bright
and touched a winter-weary world
with snow and ice delight.**

—Lucille Crumley

Beautiful, Beautiful Snow

Nelle Hardgrove

A winter world's a soft-white world
of drifts and glistening flakes
and boughs and overhangings high
and sculptured pristine lakes.
And often in this magnitude
of soft-white driven snow
are footprints small, belonging to
some creature on the go,
who stood and smelled the crisp, clear air
and then tracked upon his way . . .
excited by the wonderworld
that held the land in sway.

O winter world, O soft-white world,
in you I see God's touch
and feel that He created you
for those He loves so much.

When Winter Comes

Nora M. Bozeman

When Winter comes and cloaks the land,
she holds snow crystals in her hand.
She fashions trees in fleecy white
and icicles the eaves at night.

When Winter comes and snowflakes fly
like dancing diamonds from the sky,
she coats my windowpane in lace,
where old Jack Frost has kissed her face.

When Winter comes and north winds blow,
they drift the mounds of sculptured snow;
and I, asleep in ermine arms,
dream of Winter's wondrous charms.

It's Christmastime
Harriet Feltham

It's Christmastime, it's Christmastime!
the church bells say in every chime:
a time for work and care to cease;
give praises to the Prince of Peace.

It's Christmastime, it's Christmastime!
a day for joy in every clime
to celebrate the Christ Child's birth
and foster peace upon this earth.

Fir trees will shine with glowing light
to cheer a stranger through the night
and take a hand in brotherhood
for faith, for love and all that's good.

Carols will ring through cold, crisp air
while families gather everywhere;
and up above the stars will shine
much brighter—'cause it's Christmastime!

Christmas Town
G. Farfan

For weeks, our town
    is upside-down;
excitement knows no measure.
Girls and boys, clothes and toys,
Christmas cards to treasure,
boxes, strings, deep-secret things,
a smile on every face,
the tall green tree majestically
adorned in shining grace,
bells ring brightly, caroling nightly,
spices permeate the air,
sparkling snow sets cheeks aglow—
Christmastime is everywhere.

Time swiftly steals;
    how good it feels
to have all hurry cease.
And in its stead,
    tucked warm in bed,
we find a gentle peace.

The eve is here,
    so still, so clear;
it waits the wondrous day.
While on our town
    the Lord smiles down
and listens as we pray.

Home for Christmas

Diane Skinner

We were newlyweds anticipating our first Christmas together. My husband, Mike, had been drafted into the Army and was stationed in Virginia. We had moved out East, leaving our families back in Illinois.

The approaching holidays made my heart ache for loved ones and family traditions. Each year my mom and I would spend hours baking cookies and bread to take to neighbors and relatives.

Family was everything to my father, the son of a quiet Norwegian farmer who kept his family close. Amid sleigh rides and ice-skating parties, my father and grandfather would host family dinners that included traditional Norwegian favorites. Meatballs, fruit soup, kringla, lefse, krumkake, and rice pudding with lingonberry sauce were meticulously prepared.

This year, though, I was not surrounded by relatives making holiday goodies. And with eight hundred miles of separation, I felt alone.

Sensing my disappointment, Mike revealed that he had been tucking funds away since July. He now had enough set aside to surprise me with two airline tickets. When he told me, I hugged him and shouted, "Home? We're going home!"

Each day that followed was filled with dreams of Christmas. I crossed off each day in red on the calendar. I spent hours personalizing my gifts with colored paper and ribbons. Each morning I peered into my packed suitcases, reassuring myself that I had all I'd need.

But the night before we were to leave, a blustery snowstorm dropped a foot of fresh snow around us. Living in the Blue Ridge Mountains was thrilling, but not when it snowed. Roads were treacherous, and often we were trapped.

Mike had left our car at the base of the mountain where we lived when he'd arrived home the previous night, because our long, steep driveway had been too icy to navigate. If we wanted to get to the airport, we first had to get down the hill.

Mike sighed, disappointed that his Christmas present, the trip home, was in jeopardy. "There's no way I can carry the gifts and two suitcases down that hill. It's tricky enough to walk down empty-handed."

But I wasn't about to give up that easily. "We're going home!" I announced stubbornly.

"I don't know . . ." Mike began doubtfully.

I glanced around, as if looking for help. I spotted a toboggan resting by the porch. "Thank you, God!" I quietly prayed.

"We'll sled home!" I declared. "Well, not all the way, but far enough to get us to the car to drive to the airport."

Mike's eyes widened. He was the worry-wart in the relationship, and this was definitely not the most reasonable course of action. But my excitement about the prospect won him over—although he, reasonably, preferred to hike rather than slide to the bottom of the hill.

Image © Joy Brown/Shutterstock

We carefully stacked the boxes of presents and our two suitcases on the sled. I plastered myself on top of the toboggan's full load, like a car ornament. Grabbing the side ropes, I pointed the sled downhill and shoved with my feet.

I grinned and let out a shout of glee as the sled started off, slowly building speed. Soon, however, I began to question my choice. I pulled on the rope to slow the sled, but it just raced downward faster and faster. Could I stop? Would I crash? I clung to the boxes, bouncing in the air with each bump. Icy snowflakes pummeled my face as I sliced through drifts.

I dug both knees into my bags. The sled veered to the right—uncomfortably close to the edge of a canyon below. Mike, who was trekking behind me, shouted commands, sounding anxious about the runaway sled.

I stuck out my foot to add resistance and to steer the sled to a safer course. "I'm fine! I'm fine!" I said, assuring Mike—and myself. "Almost there." The car came into sight, the sled slowing slightly as it neared the bottom of the hill.

In one final *whoosh*, the sled came to a stop—narrowly missing our car. I had made it! I collapsed on a tree stump to warm up from my ordeal while Mike dug the car out of the snow. I was triumphant. But during the drive to the airport, I began to question myself. Had I been I fearless, or reckless? Was my ordeal worth it to save Christmas?

Once we landed on the Midwest prairie, I quickly realized that this trip home for Christmas was not what I expected. It was far more. Holiday activities and traditions like lighting the Advent wreath were more meaningful after our long absence. Affection from loved ones warmed us to the core. Our family let us know that their best Christmas gift was having us near.

I knew that I was the lucky one. The love from my husband and family filled me to the brim, preparing me to return to our new home in the East. Years later, I still smile when I glance at the framed picture of me on that sled. It reminds me to take every opportunity to celebrate with loved ones. Obstacles—even a snowy mountain—may block the way, but never give up! It's worth the risk!

The Bright Dreams of Christmas

Virginia Midgett

May the bright dreams of Christmas
shine like the star so bright
that shone o'er the manger
where the Baby lay that night.

May the bright dreams of Christmas
shine like the glowing eyes
of happy little children
when Christmas morn arrives.

May you know the warmth and sweetness
of a family bound with love
in a home that's always shining
with the light from up above.

May the memory of the carols,
ringing out peace and good cheer,
keep the bright dreams of Christmas
in your heart through all the year.

Christmas Is . . .

Geo. L. Ehrman

Christmas is a lovely dream
when lights are burning low
and hearts can feel the warmth of love
before a fireplace glow.

Christmas is a star of hope
that shines in darkest night
to light the way for all mankind
so we may walk aright.

Christmas is real life itself
with faith, its counterpart—
a time when God comes close to man
with peace for every heart.

Image © age fotostock/Superstock

Winter Ballet

Beverly J. Anderson

I sit here by my window seat
and watch the snowflakes as they fall.
They cover trees in ermine wrap
and for the shrubs purl lacy shawls.

They swirl right past my windowpane—
white ballerinas twirling round.
They dance so gaily through the air,
merrily whirling, as if wound.

My heart delights in their ballet,
performed with beauty and with grace.
Last dance completed, now they fall,
the barren earth soon to replace.

All through the night the snowflakes fall.
When dawns the early morning light
we see a fluffy comforter
has blanketed the ground in white.

A Postcard Countryside

Loise Pinkerton Fritz

The gentle snow is falling;
oh, what a peaceful sight!
It glistens on the rooftops
and on the
    mountain heights.

It looks like sparkled icing
on frozen ponds
    and streams;
it dabs a touch of beauty
on boughs of evergreens.

Upon the stretching
    fence rows
that line the country fields,
the lustrous flakes are falling
as bells of evening peal.

The vacant nests in treetops
are topped with
    puffs of white;
each one's a part and parcel
of a postcard countryside.

A Christmas Memory

Deborah A. Bennett

That night before Christmas, I was five years old, and everything in our house smelled of sweet potato pie, sage and cornbread turkey stuffing, and coconut and chocolate cakes baking in the oven. My brother, sisters, and I were sent to play in the living room while our mother made magic happen. As far as I knew, fairy dust and wishes made Christmas smell like that, made it feel warm like yellow blankets pulled up under our chins, made it feel like kisses on our foreheads—made it feel like love.

While tiny white lights glowed soft on the Christmas tree like stars in a clear, black sky, I'd pinch one bulb between my fingers, pulling it into the little wooden window of the creche hanging on a shadowy bottom limb. The light fell on Mary cradling her little baby, on Joseph holding his lamp beside the manger, on shepherds kneeling on golden hay. It was what I did every year while no one else was watching, I thought. Only God, the holy family, and me. Outside the windows, snow fell quietly while streetlights pinged into little moons. Bundles of people slid along the sidewalk, and pigeons, every now and then, *coo-cooed* out on the ledge. The twilight sky was pink and orange and full of twinkling flakes and wind. And I felt safe and warm and exactly where I ought to have been, even trying to stay out from underfoot of Mama's Christmas Eve chores.

My little sister held her baby doll in her arms, a pink bottle full of water dripping down its rosebud mouth. My big brother drove his toy cars along the baseboards and up and down the walls. And my big sister knelt beside the record player, listening to Nat King Cole sing the holiday in.

I lay on my stomach reading my favorites— *Alice in Wonderland*, *Treasure Island*, and *Pippi Longstocking*, wondering what it would be like to be a pirate princess at Christmastime. Our gray-striped tabby cat lay on his back, asleep and dreaming, humming like the radiator and, I imagined, swatting dream-mice or hiding in the tall dream-grass. Momma put the ham in the oven, and the smell hypnotized me as it filtered down the hall. And I could feel it on my cheeks, sweet and warm beside the cakes baking, and the onions frying in the skillet for the stuffing, and the vanilla in the bowl of sweet potatoes.

It was bathtime after that, with the smell of Ivory soap and almond-and-cherry-scented lotion. Then I was tucked in between cool, white sheets beside my sister, who folded her hands, staring up at the ceiling, a candle behind her eyes, whispering some sweet secret to the dark.

It was the middle of the night when I slid out of the warm bed and onto the cold hardwood floor. I remember half sleepwalking to the bathroom door when, out of the corner of my eye, I saw her. My mother sat assembling the biggest, most beautiful Victorian dollhouse I had ever seen.

She froze in place as I passed her like a ghost. All was hazy and happy, like wandering into a dream. And I floated back to bed that Christmas night, shifting in between pillows and teddy bears and blankets, drifting down to sleep. My sisters rested soundly, *there* and *there*. My brother was as

close as across the wall. My mother made magic only rooms away. In my dream, I was Alice, falling through the looking glass. On tiptoe I wandered in a garden, looking up at the sky. The snow whispered down between the stars, on the heads of trees, on the wings of red birds and butterflies by the stream, and in the cups of tulips by the garden gate—where I lifted my arms in the cool dream air, where I waved my hands and waited.

Christmas Tree Neighbors

Pamela Love

Through an angel's golden wings,
I see a snowman peek
at reindeer that are prancing by
a small brown donkey meek.

And there's a boy of gingerbread
beside a snow-white dove,
next to a cuddly teddy bear
whose dress was made with love.

These ornaments are so different,
and yet each year I see
how much they brighten up
   my house
by being neighborly.

Garnished

Faith E. Kessi

I hung an ornament on my tree;
in its shimmering beauty I seemed to see
gold, which the Magi laid at the feet
of the newborn Christ Child,
   tiny and sweet.

A shining angel I put in place
and thought that I saw in its lovely face
peace, and I heard the echoing song
"good will to men" from the
   heavenly throng.

To the topmost bough I fastened a star
and remembered the journey
   from lands afar—

three kings and the light that guided them
to the humble stable in Bethlehem.

Each candle clipped to the branches there,
twinkling and glowing a message to share
that none be in darkness, for great
   is the light
brought by the Christ Child that first
   Noel night.

Not only the tree had I decked
   Christmas Eve,
but my heart was made ready the Child
   to receive.

Legacy
Eileen Burnett

I saw Christmas.
'Twas a shining light,
not from a star
deep in the night,
not from a planet
far in the skies.
The light I beheld was
in a little girl's eyes.
So, as she gazed at
the candles and tree,
the faith that is
Christmas
was kindled in me!

Her baby delight carols out in surprise
as the colorful lights twinkle back in her eyes;
she "oohs" and she "ahhs,"
toddling closer to see
what makes it so pretty—
her first Christmas tree.
—ELVERIA BLUST

On Christmas Morning
Robert D. Little

A star may glow in its orbit;
moons may wax and wane;
the wondrous sight of Northern Lights
shall come and go again.
But never a shining light
has brightened land or sea
as that which lies in children's eyes
around the Christmas tree!

Through My Window

The Christmas Box

Pamela Kennedy

When you come to grandparenting late, you have lots of time to observe your peers giving gifts to their grandchildren. One grandfather I know buys things that are far too advanced for his grandsons—an electric train for a three-year-old, complicated remote control cars for a four-year-old. Then, when the little tykes keep slamming the delicate engines down on the tracks or repeatedly crash the remote-controlled monster trucks into a concrete wall, it usually doesn't end well. Papa gets frustrated, and the tots are in tears.

A close friend of mine creates lovely dresses and coats for her granddaughters. They are made from delicate fabrics and feature intricately crafted stitching, seed pearls, rhinestone buttons, lace, and ribbons. The girls look beautiful in them. But after the obligatory holiday photos, the precious garments are packed away in the closet as treasured keepsakes.

Most of us recognize that this kind of gift-giving, while obviously rooted in love, is primarily because the grandparent probably never received, but always coveted, electric trains and remote-controlled cars or beautiful, handcrafted clothes and can't wait to bestow them on a grandchild.

I'm trying to resist this inclination. Last Christmas, our only grandson, Henry, was just a bit over two. I spent lots of time searching for the perfect age-appropriate gifts to tuck under the tree and into his stocking. I particularly wanted things that would spark his creativity. I eschewed toys that were clearly marketed to promote some commercial behemoth or multi-million dollar Hollywood movie franchise. I avoided toys that required a handful of batteries, repeated inane questions, played irritating jingles, or blasted ear-splitting sirens.

I suppose you could say I was something of a toy snob, although I prefer to characterize it as being a purist. I purchased colorful wooden puzzles, books, tubs of Play-Doh, a mat with roads for driving small cars, and a child-sized kitchen, complete with little pots and pans. Each gift was wrapped with care and tied with colorful ribbons. Henry loved them all . . . especially the paper and ribbons!

When the packages were all opened and we adults were busy preparing dinner, Henry puttered around with his new toys. Now and then he brought his uncles a car or a puzzle piece for inspection or adjustment, but for the most part he seemed happily occupied. I was feeling particularly virtuous about my gifting choices. Of course he was happy, I mused. He was busy with all the interesting toys I had so thoughtfully chosen. But perhaps I shouldn't have been quite so quick to give myself a pat on the back.

When I eventually went to check on Henry, wondering which of my gifts had so completely captivated him, I was surprised to find him sitting in a sturdy cardboard box next to his play mat.

"Look, Grammy," he exclaimed with a grin, "I have a big truck. I'm taking my cars on a trip."

He held up his hands, each fist gripping a small plastic car. "Brrrrrm. Brrrrmm. Going on a trip, cars!" he continued.

"That's great, Henry, but what about your kitchen, or maybe this cool puzzle with the animals? Want to play with these?"

"Nope. I like my truck. My cars like it too."

Later that evening Henry emptied the box of cars and filled it with his stuffed animals and a blanket. "We're going on an airplane," he announced. "Kitty wants to go up in the sky."

The following day, the box was a cement mixer, a fire truck, and a spaceship and had been enjoyed so much it needed to be reinforced with duct tape. When we loaded up the family's car, Henry wept until we packed his battered box too.

A week later I spent the day visiting Henry. He made me "cookies" on his play stove, and we directed the traffic around on the play mat. We enjoyed some happy hours doing puzzles and reading books. But over in the corner, tucked between a bookcase and the wall, I spied the box. There was a pie plate taped to the front flap (Henry told

Image © Sandra Cunningham/Shutterstock

me that was his steering wheel) and two toilet paper tubes with orange tissue paper stuck in their ends fastened to the back (rocket engines, said Henry).

I'm thinking I don't need to worry about Henry's imagination. And I probably don't need to spend a boatload of time or money searching for creative toys either. I wonder if there is some place where you can just get lots of different sized boxes, oh, and toilet paper tubes, and maybe some duct tape. With all of that, by the time he's three, Henry will probably create his own robot or computer or even a time machine!

First Christmas
Gail Brook Burket

Your mind will not recall this tree,
adorned with twinkling dots of light,
the holly wreaths and mistletoe,
and voices singing, "Holy Night."
But we shall treasure through the years
your baby coos of rapt surprise,
your dimpled fingers reaching out,
and glowing wonder in your eyes.

His First Christmas
Harriet Whipple

We bought him gifts this Christmas,
and so did others too,
and all were so excited
to see just what he'd do.

We brought him downstairs early,
just barely did he wake.
The cameras were all ready
for the pictures we would take.

In wee blue-striped pajamas,
he posed with a smile
and blinked at all the flashes
in a way to beguile.

Then the Christmas tree lights
attracted our small boy;
his shining eyes sparkled,
and he chuckled with joy.

He reached out to touch them,
but Mom said, *No, no,*
and showed him the presents
all piled up below.

Then each one was opened,
revealing toy after toy—
but it was the wrappings
that thrilled our small boy!

A Gift of Love

Dona Maxey

With five dollars in my pocket and twenty people on my Christmas list, I wandered the aisles of our local Ben Franklin store. *I can spend twenty-five cents apiece*, I mentally calculated. It was Christmas in the early 1960s, and my task, although difficult, was not impossible. I began selecting items carefully, matching each to a name on my list.

Then I saw it. High on a shelf in the housewares department sat a shiny black ceramic cookie jar, a fairly convincing replica of a cast-iron cooking stove. It took my breath away. *That is perfect for Mother!* I thought, all the devotion of my young heart surfacing. But the price was almost half of the total amount I possessed. Discouraged, I trudged on. Somehow, nothing else seemed appropriate for her. Returning to Housewares, I lingered longingly, resisting the lure of its shiny finish, looking carefully at my lengthy Christmas list. Then, gingerly, I lifted it from the shelf and placed it in my shopping cart.

Now, retracing my steps, I returned some previously chosen items. My shopping for others had to begin again. Here was a blue pocket comb for ten cents and a package of white handkerchiefs for twenty-five cents. Each handkerchief could serve as a gift for a separate person. A display of small porcelain vases and figurines bearing the required price tags caught my eye. I selected several.

On down the list I worked until, at last, a gift for each of the twenty family members had been found. The cost, including cookie jar and tax, totaled slightly under five dollars. Triumphant, I bore my purchases home and wrapped them, taking special care to protect the black ceramic cookie jar.

Christmas Eve, when Mother unwrapped my gift to her, she exclaimed, "Dona, you spent most of your money on me!" Shyly, I threw my arms around her, hoping my gift would somehow convey the love and affection I felt for her but seemed unable to adequately express.

Many years passed. My parents moved to various parts of the country, even abroad. I married and raised my own family. Then one day, while visiting with Mother in her kitchen, I spied a familiar black shape sitting on the counter. No longer shiny, but scratched and dull, it had lost the distinguishing markings that made it resemble a cast-iron cooking stove. In fact, had I not been previously acquainted with it, I probably could not have guessed what it was.

"Do you still have that old thing?" I gasped, pleased but astonished that it had not been long ago broken or discarded.

"Why, yes," replied Mother nostalgically, recalling a memory only she and I now shared. "You gave it to me one year for Christmas."

With a mother's intuition, she had sensed the significance of my clumsy, inexpensive gift, cherishing it above many nicer presents I presented to her later.

Just as the affection motivating a childish gift touched an earthly mother's heart, so the heart of our heavenly Father is moved when we offer to Him a full measure of devotion. Long ago, the Wise Men brought gifts to Jesus. Will you join them and give your devotion as a gift to Him?

Practice Time!

Winnie Barnett

Christmastime is drawing nigh;
rehearsal time is here
for concerts and for programs
that bring the message dear!

This year, Sue's an angel, so
she needs a costume white.
Mother's busy stitching
one with tinsel bright!

Brother Bill's a shepherd
with robe and rugged stick.

Downstairs, Father's fashioning
one to do the trick!

Mary Jane and Timmy
are practicing their part,
reciting it so often
it would warm most any heart!

Soon we'll gather round the stage
to hear the glad refrain
of old, familiar carols—
it's practice time again!

Pageantry

Gracia Grindal

It's Mary's song of how the mighty fall.
Her small voice quavers through the
        waiting church—
a little girl in blue with a shiny foil
halo around her head. She makes her speech
in words that comprehend what she cannot
before the bathrobed shepherds kneeling there.
"The proud shall be brought low."
        She gets it right.
Suddenly, overhead's a neon star;
a baby cries; the congregation smiles.
The pantomime of life before us works.
They act the story out, the miracle
becomes them. Rulers have not seen the likes
of this before: cattle, wise men kneel;
the make-believe before us is made real.

Nativity Scene—
School Hall

Gladys McKee

There will be a tinsel star
above a straw-filled manger;
there will good St. Joseph stand,
firm against all danger;
Mary, blue-gowned, sweet, will hold
the little Infant Jesus;
angels, rosy-cheeked and small,
will sing their songs to please us.
You will look on smilingly,
nodding side to side;
I shall need a kerchief
to catch a tear of pride;
and the miracle of Christmas
will be, for us, each minute
the little donkey stands serene,
with *our* Jimmy in it.

The Story of a Song

Jingle Bells

Pamela Kennedy

It will surprise most people to learn that this holiday favorite wasn't actually written as a New England Christmas carol. In fact, musicologists believe it was a romantic jingle, most likely composed in Savannah, Georgia—in the summer! The carol's unusual origins, however, might be quite fitting since its creator had a reputation as something of a rebel and rogue.

After running away from boarding school to sail the high seas, James Lord Pierpont eventually returned to his New England home. There he married Millicent Cowee with whom he had two children between 1845 and 1849. Unable to resist his urge for adventure, James soon abandoned his young family to the care of his father and headed west to seek his fortune in the San Francisco gold rush. In 1852, after his business burned to the ground, James left California, but did not return to Massachusetts. He moved instead to Savannah, Georgia, taking a position as organist and music director at the Unitarian Church, where his brother, John Pierpont Jr., served as minister. James' career as a popular songwriter began that year with a number called "The Returned Californian," one verse of which offers a glimpse into his motives:

Oh! I'm going far away but I don't
    know where I'll go,
I oughter travel homeward but they'll
    laugh at me I know;
For I told 'em when I started I was
    bound to make a pile,
But if they could only see me now I
    rather guess they'd smile.

After Millicent's death in 1856, James married Eliza Jane Purse, the daughter of Savannah's mayor. And it was in August of that year that he published his jingle, "The One-Horse Open Sleigh." About eighteen months later the publisher changed the title to "Jingle Bells," hoping to boost sales, but it wasn't until the end of the Civil War that it gained national popularity.

Almost a century later, on December 16, 1965, "Jingle Bells" became the first Christmas song performed in outer space! Astronauts Wally Schirra and Tom Stafford, aboard *Gemini* 6, sent the following message to Mission Control: "We have an object, looks like a satellite going from north to south, probably in a polar orbit. . . . I see a command module and eight smaller modules in front. . . . The command pilot of the command module is wearing a red suit." Then the astronauts pulled out an inch-long harmonica and sleigh bells they had smuggled aboard and serenaded Mission Control with their rendition of "Jingle Bells."

Jingle Bells

Lyrics and melody by James Lord Pierpont (1822–1893)

Bits & Pieces

And suddenly there was
with the angel a multitude
of the heavenly host praising
God, and saying, Glory to God
in the highest, and on earth
peace, good will toward men.
—*Luke 2:13–14*

The angels sang sweet carols first
while shepherds watched their sheep;
they sang in voices soft and low
to let the Baby sleep.

Glad shepherds heard them in the fields
and saw the star on high;
and then perhaps they joined the song—
the world's first lullaby.
—*June Masters Bacher*

Christmas Eve was a night of song that wrapped itself about you like a shawl. But it warmed more than your body. It warmed your heart . . . filled it, too, with melody that would last forever.
—Bess Streeter Aldrich

There's nothing like getting together with friends at Christmastime to celebrate with music the incredible reality of the Savior's birth.
—Steven Curtis Chapman

Hear the carolers sing their songs, their candles bright and voices strong. Within their hearts is Christmas glee as they gather round the tree.
—Joseph F. Daniel

The carolers are singing across the world again. Their joyous words go winging in jubilant reply to choirs of angels bringing glad tidings from on high.
—Gail Brook Burket

Come out and join the caroling, good friends and neighbors jolly— come! Let us wreath the world in song more brilliant than the holly!
—Rowena Bastin Bennett

Merry Julekake!

Anne Kennedy Brady

Because I grew up in a military family, holiday traditions and locations often had to be adjusted. My parents were eager, however, to provide my brothers and me with some stability in the midst of regular uprooting, so they determined that Christmas would remain relatively the same no matter where we lived. Thus, Christmas morning has always followed the strict schedule of stocking gifts, breakfast, then tree gifts. And breakfast is always Julekake.

Julekake is a Norwegian sweet bread stuffed with nuts and candied fruit. Family legend recounts that over a hundred years ago, a loose-lipped Norse cousin gave up her secret recipe for this Yuletide breakfast treat and Great-Grandma proceeded to make it every year thereafter. When her daughter married, the recipe went with her.

My grandma, possessing a charming streak of stubborn creativity, put her own stamp on her mother's tradition. The original bread was a pallid hue hovering between ecru and nude. Grandma jazzed it up by adding several drops of red food coloring, then embellishing each loaf with drizzled powdered sugar frosting and a line of five candied cherry halves down the middle. The results brought to mind sunburnt bellies bursting out of tidy, buttoned waistcoats.

My father's childhood memories prominently feature this festive, rosy bread. It just wasn't Christmas without it. So when he married my mother, he handed her the recipe, sheepishly requesting that they continue the Julekake legacy. Eager to make their first Christmas perfect, Mom dutifully stocked up on red food coloring,

tracked down the requisite candied fruits, peels, and nuts, and set to work. How hard could it be?

That first batch has become family lore. First, she promptly knocked over an open bottle of red food coloring. "It looked like a crime scene," she recalls.

Then, the kneading. At every turn, the stiff dough ejected a candied cherry here or a walnut there. After vainly trying to secure the escapees, Mom, close to tears, called her mother-in-law to admit defeat.

"Oh, that's what it always does, dear," Grandma replied, airily. "Just shove them back in!"

Unconvinced, Mom nonetheless persevered and at last slid the shaped and twice-raised loaves into the oven. When they emerged, fragrant and delightfully pink, she was as relieved as Dad was thrilled. "It's really Christmas!" he declared. And despite her exhausted realization that the ordeal would become an annual one, Mom had to agree that, yes, it really was.

Now, every year, Mom prepares the loaves a few days in advance, and on Christmas morning Dad mans the oven. Slicing each loaf with a surgeon's care, he toasts the pieces to perfection under the broiler. He calls this "making Julekake," prompting Mom to smirk and roll her eyes. As we all breathe in the sweet, yeasty fragrance and lick the last buttery crumbs from our fingers, we pronounce this year's batch the best Mom—or Dad—has ever made.

And it's true. For me, this year's batch will always be the best because, although my brothers and I are now grown and living thousands of miles apart, every time we sit together at the family table sharing warm bread on Christmas morning, I am once again the little sister, cozy in my flannel PJs, embraced by love.

As my husband and I consider growing our own family, there may come a day when we cannot make a holiday trip from Chicago to Seattle.

While some things about Christmas morning will necessarily change, you can bet I'll start each December tracking down candied cherries and digging out this recipe. After all, it just isn't Christmas without Julekake.

Grandma's Julekake

(Arlene Kennedy via Pamela Kennedy)

4 ¼-ounce packages active dry yeast	3 eggs
2 cups whole milk, warmed to 105° to 115°F	½ teaspoon salt
10 cups all-purpose flour, divided	1½ cups candied cherry halves, divided
1½ cups plus 2 tablespoons granulated sugar, divided	1 cup raisins
Red food coloring, optional	1 cup citron
½ cup plus 1 to 2 tablespoons softened butter, divided	1 cup walnut pieces
	2 cups confectioners' sugar
	1 teaspoon almond extract
	3 to 4 tablespoons milk

In a large bowl, combine yeast and warm milk; let stand until yeast is dissolved, about 5 minutes. Add 3 cups flour, 2 tablespoons sugar, and a few drops food coloring, if desired. Mix well; cover lightly with plastic wrap and let rise 1 hour in a warm place.

In a medium bowl, cream remaining sugar, ½ cup butter, eggs, and salt until fluffy. With a wooden spoon, mix in 1 cup candied cherry halves, raisins, citron, and walnut pieces. Add batter to risen dough and blend with wooden spoon or dough hook. Add flour, ½ cup at a time, until mixture is stiff. Knead by hand, adding flour just until dough is smooth and elastic and no longer sticky. Divide into 4 equal portions and mold

each into an oval loaf. Place 2 loaves on each of 2 lightly greased cookie sheets. Lightly butter tops of loaves. Cover with a towel and let rise in a warm place until doubled, about 1 to 2 hours.

Preheat oven to 300°F. Bake until a toothpick inserted in the middle comes out dry, 45 minutes to 1 hour. Remove from oven and place bread on cooling racks; allow to cool.

In a small bowl, combine confectioners' sugar and almond extract; stir in milk 1 tablespoon at a time, adding until icing is spreadable but not stiff. Spread icing over cooled loaves; add a row of candied cherry halves down the center of each loaf while frosting is still soft. Store in a tightly closed container. Makes 4 loaves.

Family Recipes

Savory Christmas Cheese Bread

3 cups all-purpose flour

2 teaspoons baking powder

1¼ teaspoons salt

1 cup freshly grated Parmesan cheese

1 cup shredded sharp Cheddar or mozzarella

4 tablespoons butter, softened

1 large garlic clove, crushed and minced, optional

½ cup finely chopped scallion tops or chives, lightly packed; or green bell peppers

½ cup finely chopped sun-dried tomatoes, diced red bell peppers, or diced pimientos

4 large eggs

½ cup whole milk

Preheat oven to 350°F. In a large bowl, combine flour, baking powder, salt, cheeses, and softened butter; mix until well combined and crumbly. Mix in garlic, scallion tops, and sun-dried tomatoes; set aside. In a small bowl, whisk together eggs and milk. Set aside 1 tablespoon of mixture. Add remaining egg mixture to dry ingredients. Fold just until dry ingredients are moistened; the batter will be stiff. Scrape the batter into a greased 9-inch round cake pan or casserole dish.

Using wet fingers, spread batter to edges of pan, with edges slightly higher than center. Brush top of loaf with reserved egg mixture. Bake until top is light golden brown and a toothpick inserted into the center comes out clean, about 35 to 40 minutes. Remove from oven; run a knife around edge of the pan to loosen sides. Turn out onto a rack to cool. Serve warm, toasted, or at room temperature. Makes one 9-inch round loaf.

Gingerbread

1½ cups all-purpose flour
¾ teaspoon ground ginger
¾ teaspoon ground cinnamon
½ teaspoon baking powder
½ teaspoon baking soda
½ teaspoon salt

½ cup butter, softened
¼ cup brown sugar
1 egg
½ cup light molasses
½ cup boiling water
   Confectioners' sugar

Preheat oven to 350°F. Sift together flour, ginger, cinnamon, baking powder, baking soda, and salt. Set aside. In a large bowl, cream butter and brown sugar until light and fluffy. Beat in egg and molasses. Add flour mixture and water; stir just until combined. Pour batter into a greased and floured 9-inch round pan. Bake until a toothpick inserted into center of cake comes out clean, 30 to 35 minutes. Cool in pan on wire rack for 10 minutes. Remove from pan and serve warm or let cool. Dust with confectioners' sugar just before serving. Makes one 9-inch round loaf.

Leek and Bacon Flatbread

6 slices bacon, chopped
1 medium leek, white and light
     green parts thinly sliced and
     rinsed thoroughly
   Kosher salt
   Freshly ground black pepper

   Olive oil
1 pound prepared pizza dough
2 cups grated Gruyère cheese
     (about 4 ounces)
   Freshly grated nutmeg

Preheat oven to 500°F. Cook the bacon in a medium skillet over medium heat until crisp, about 12 minutes. Remove to paper towels to drain. Cook leeks in bacon drippings, stirring frequently, until tender but not browned, about 5 minutes. Season with salt and pepper; remove to paper towels to drain. Place pizza dough in the center of a lightly oiled 12-by-17-inch baking sheet; gradually press and stretch dough to fit the pan. Sprinkle cheese evenly on top, followed by leeks and bacon. Bake until crust is golden brown, 11 to 15 minutes. Sprinkle with nutmeg. Transfer to a cutting board and cut into pieces. Makes 8 to 10 servings.

Gingerbread Memory

Pamela Love

I've lost count of the gingerbread houses
(each perfect in every way)
that I've decorated in years past.
But what do I see today?

This marshmallow roof's collapsing;
that cinnamon chimney's askew.
The licorice windows are missing;
quick, pass me icing for glue!

A dozen gumdrops have been squashed flat;
the sprinkles have spilled on my floor.
And I see only two or three candy canes
when there should be twice that or more.

But while judges may not give it prizes,
I'm prizing the giggles I hear.
With my little ones' help I am building
a gingerbread memory this year.

Christmas Has a Secret

Michael Drury

There is an old legend about Christmas bread that I cherish. It goes something like this: Anything given to others at Christmastime is holy bread; the act of dividing it multiplies it. At Christmas, one loaf would be enough to feed the whole world. I believe in this legend, for I have seen it happen.

I had spent months writing a book that I deeply believed in, and I had become temporarily poor in the process. I had planned to scrape along on savings, but a book always takes longer than you expect. There are also stretches when you are sure that the work is no good and that you must have been mad to attempt it.

I was in such a spell as Christmas drew near. There was little I could do to make merry except send a few cards. Then I received a card from someone three thousand miles away with a check for five dollars enclosed. Three years earlier I had given this friend five dollars in a small emergency. Now she was able to return it and did so gladly. I'm not really one for "signs and wonders," but that little check lay on my worktable for days, curiously spurring my faith in the work I was doing.

There is a man who has been kind to me, and I had hoped to buy him a book. But was that practical? I rather needed that five dollars, and the man wouldn't expect a gift. We weren't on that sort of basis. Yet the complete surprise of it was part of the pleasure, and anyway, there was the matter of holy bread. I bought the book and wrapped it in bright paper. I felt immensely happy every time I looked at it.

Two days later another greeting card arrived with a ten-dollar bill folded into it—in appreciation of a small service I had once performed for a neighbor. "Christmas bread!" I thought. "It really does multiply." Then, I heard of a young couple in great financial difficulty, and I sent the ten dollars to them. I wasn't actually poor or hungry, and I knew what an unexpected boost can mean far beyond its cash value. After all, I had just received two of them myself. It was Christmas bread. It had watered my soul; now it was time to pass it on.

On the afternoon before Christmas, I sat down with a cup of tea and a piece of fruitcake and began opening the day's mail. In a letter from my sister was a check for one hundred dollars. She knew of my book, and it was her way of saying, "Keep on." I sat looking at it for a full minute. A bit later I tore open a letter from a bank and learned that a loan had been repaid to my mother's estate—enough for me to live on for several months. I could now finish my job with ease. Holy bread, indeed. When you share it, you cannot get rid of the stuff. How can I not believe the old story? Legends become legends because they are rooted in deep laws of life.

Outside a village church in Switzerland one cold winter night, a tired man waited for the evening service to begin. He had come a long way, and the church was dark. He began to wonder if any service was planned—despite the ringing of the bells that had lured him there.

But then, through the forest, he saw pinpricks of light bobbing and moving toward him. The congregation was assembling, each group carrying its own lighted lantern. After a few had arrived, the weary man followed them and sank down on a pew in the shadowy church. As more and more people came, each hanging his lantern on an iron hook in the wall, the shadows retreated and the church began to glow with light.

After the service, the traveler stopped to ask the pastor about this unique method of illuminating the church.

"But it is the only means we have, monsieur," the clergyman replied. "In the 1500s, when many of these churches were built, it was too costly for the church to supply candles. It was usual for each family to carry a lantern. Our church has chosen to carry on the old custom. If someone does not come, we all feel it. The church is darker by one lantern."

The traveler thanked his host and went away, knowing at last what he must do to regain his joy in living. He had to carry his own lamp.

In the dark night when the earth sleeps, Christmas trees bloom with light and color, the crisp air is scented with hearth fires and spices, and houses are polished and decorated. Bells ring, voices are raised in laughter and hymns, and people salute one another and exchange beribboned packages— all because human beings make it so. Nature does this sort of thing the rest of the year; at Christmastime, it's up to us.

Do at least one totally unselfish thing for someone, even if he or she doesn't deserve it—perhaps especially if he doesn't. Take a poinsettia to that tiresome neighbor or that couple in the next block you usually avoid. Invite just one person over for coffee and cookies, if that's all the time or money you can spare.

Create a spot of beauty. Spend a dollar or two for something decorative—a bunch of greens, a pair of bayberry candles, a box of gleaming ornaments—and arrange it in your home. Make a paper chain the way you did at school and loop it in front of a mirror or crisscross it over a window.

It may sound absurd to say that anything so public as Christmas has a secret, but it does and this is it: It is necessary to light your own lantern in the darkness. The customs must be kept— guarded and cared for—if Christmas is to take on life for us. The bread is offered, but it has to be eaten—and shared.

The Singing Stars
Marjorie Wilson

All the stars tonight are singing,
as this midnight now draws near.
So too the bells of heaven were ringing
on that midnight, sweet and clear.

As we hear again the story,
that with telling ne'er grows dim,
our hearts are stirred by sweetness and we
kneel in worship to Him.

Through the ages, the refrain comes,
wondrous now, as it was then;
and the silver stars keep singing,
"Peace on earth! Good will toward men!"

The Christmas Star
Nancy Byrd Turner

High in the heavens, a single star
of pure, imperishable light;
out on the desert, strange and far,
dim riders riding through the night:
above a hilltop a sudden song
like silver trumpets rang down from the sky—
and all to welcome One so young,
he scarce could lift a cry!

Stars rise and set; that star shines on.
Songs fail, but still that music beats
through all the ages come and gone,
in lane and field and city streets.
And we who catch the Christmas gleam,
watching with children on the hill,
we know, we know it is no dream—
He stands among us still!

The Miracle
Lucy H. King Smith

Ring out, sweet Christmas bells, and fling
a message deep to every thing—
tell of a Savior, whose dear birth
brings love, good will, and peace on earth.

High in the heav'ns, the mystery lies
in awe 'neath beauteous starlit skies.
The shepherds on Judea's plain
heard first the word of Jesus' reign.

A star aflame did lead the way
to where the Babe—the Christ Child—lay.
The light that shone o'er Bethlehem
became a heavenly diadem.

In manger sheltered—lowly, mild—
a vision lay, a newborn Child;
in life to shine and lift earth's night,
a sacred beacon of rare light.

Celestial radiance hovered there;
glad tidings went out everywhere.
Angelic beauty touched the place;
God's halo crowned a little face.

A lowly, little Boy, He came
unknown, unheralded by fame;
and yet the world its debt now owes
for His compassion in life's woes.

But for His birth, His gentle mien,
the earth to depths would sink again;
His star in glory did arise
to point the way to Paradise.

The Christmas Song
W. L. Stidger

The Christmas song was in the air,
its subtle charm felt everywhere:
from Rome and Athens in their pride
to every little countryside
when o'er Judea's little town
the angel hosts came singing down.

The Christmas song is in the air;
one hears it ringing everywhere:
he hears it on the busy streets
from lips of everyone he meets
and knows that still o'er every town
the angel hosts are singing down.

Love's Offering
Phillip Gregory

What shall I bring Thee, O little Stranger,
cradled with straw in a Judean manger?
No gold nor myrrh, nor incense rare,
have I, dear Babe, with Thee to share;
but Thou dost treasure the gift I bring,
my heart, love's dearest offering.

Jesus Foretold and Mary's Praise
LUKE 1:26–33, 46–55

AND IN THE SIXTH MONTH the angel Gabriel was sent from God unto a city of Galilee, named Nazareth, To a virgin espoused to a man whose name was Joseph, of the house of David; and the virgin's name was Mary.

And the angel came in unto her, and said, Hail, thou that art highly favoured, the Lord is with thee: blessed art thou among women.

And when she saw him, she was troubled at his saying, and cast in her mind what manner of salutation this should be.

And the angel said unto her, Fear not, Mary: for thou hast found favour with God. And, behold, thou shalt conceive in thy womb, and bring forth a son, and shalt call his name JESUS. He shall be great, and shall be called the Son of the Highest: and the Lord God shall give unto him the throne of his father David: And he shall reign over the house of Jacob for ever; and of his kingdom there shall be no end. . . .

And Mary said, My soul doth magnify the Lord, And my spirit hath rejoiced in God my Saviour. For he hath regarded the low estate of his handmaiden: for, behold, from henceforth all generations shall call me blessed. For he that is mighty hath done to me great things; and holy is his name. And his mercy is on them that fear him from generation to generation. He hath shewed strength with his arm; he hath scattered the proud in the imagination of their hearts. He hath put down the mighty from their seats, and exalted them of low degree. He hath filled the hungry with good things; and the rich he hath sent empty away. He hath helped his servant Israel, in remembrance of his mercy; As he spake to our fathers, to Abraham, and to his seed for ever.

Angels Appear to the Shepherds
LUKE 2:8–20

AND THERE WERE IN THE SAME COUNTRY shepherds abiding in the field, keeping watch over their flock by night. And, lo, the angel of the Lord came upon them, and the glory of the Lord shone round about them: and they were sore afraid.

And the angel said unto them, Fear not: for, behold, I bring you good tidings of great joy, which shall be to all people. For unto you is born this day in the city of David a Saviour, which is Christ the Lord. And this shall be a sign unto you; Ye shall find the babe wrapped in swaddling clothes, lying in a manger.

And suddenly there was with the angel a multitude of the heavenly host praising God, and saying, Glory to God in the highest, and on earth peace, good will toward men.

And it came to pass, as the angels were gone away from them into heaven, the shepherds said one to another, Let us now go even unto Bethlehem, and see this thing which is come to pass, which the Lord hath made known unto us.

And they came with haste, and found Mary, and Joseph, and the babe lying in a manger. And when they had seen it, they made known abroad the saying which was told them concerning this child.

And all they that heard it wondered at those things which were told them by the shepherds.

But Mary kept all these things, and pondered them in her heart.

And the shepherds returned, glorifying and praising God for all the things that they had heard and seen, as it was told unto them.

The Wise Men from the East
MATTHEW 2:1–12

NOW WHEN JESUS WAS BORN in Bethlehem of Judaea in the days of Herod the king, behold, there came wise men from the east to Jerusalem, Saying, Where is he that is born King of the Jews? for we have seen his star in the east, and are come to worship him. When Herod the king had heard these things, he was troubled, and all Jerusalem with him. And when he had gathered all the chief priests and scribes of the people together, he demanded of them where Christ should be born.

And they said unto him, In Bethlehem of Judaea: for thus it is written by the prophet, And thou Bethlehem, in the land of Juda, art not the least among the princes of Juda: for out of thee shall come a Governor, that shall rule my people Israel.

Then Herod, when he had privily called the wise men, enquired of them diligently what time the star appeared. And he sent them to Bethlehem, and said, Go and search diligently for the young child; and when ye have found him, bring me word again, that I may come and worship him also.

When they had heard the king, they departed; and, lo, the star, which they saw in the east, went before them, till it came and stood over where the young child was.

When they saw the star, they rejoiced with exceeding great joy.

And when they were come into the house, they saw the young child with Mary his mother, and fell down, and worshipped him: and when they had opened their treasures, they presented unto him gifts; gold, and frankincense and myrrh.

And being warned of God in a dream that they should not return to Herod, they departed into their own country another way.

After Bethlehem
Myra Scovel

"You must return by another road,"
the Wise Men heard God say.
Another road? The old road
was the known, the safest way.
But the kings had been to Bethlehem,
had knelt as humble men,
and nothing, after Bethlehem,
could be the same again.

The Kings of the East
Katharine Lee Bates

The kings of the East are riding
tonight to Bethlehem.
The sunset glows, dividing;
the kings of the East are riding,
a star their journey guiding,
gleaming with gold and gem.
The kings of the East are riding
tonight to Bethlehem.

There beams above the manger
the child-face of a star;
amid the stars a stranger,
it beams above the manger;
what means this ether-ranger
to pause where poor folk are?
There beams above a manger
the child-face of a star.

The Light of Bethlehem
Thomas Curtis Clark

Above a world entrapped by fear,
there shone a silver star.
The doubters saw it not, nor cared;
the men of faith, from far,
knew that the Light of love looked down
and followed it through field and town.

Through desert lands they made their way
past mountains bleak and wild;
they came to humble Bethlehem
and found a little Child.
Their hearts were stirred: their feet had trod
a road to peace—they learned of God!

Our hearts are broken by the years,
but still there shines a star
above a little manger-home.
Oh, that we might, from far,
retrace our steps through fear and night
to faith and hope, and Bethl'hem's light!

Christmas Travelers

Dr. Ralph F. Wilson

Christmas brings to mind the story of travelers propelled by the unhurried rhythm of their animals: "We three kings of Orient are bearing gifts we traverse afar, field and fountain, moor and mountain, following yonder star."

Why did these Wise Men undertake such a journey?

A tall astronomer, advisor to the Persian king, springs from his midnight vigil in the palace courtyard. "Caspar, come! Look along the rod I've sighted toward the constellation of the Jews." Caspar peers into the blackness. "Do you see it? That brilliant star is new tonight! It must signify the birth of a mighty King."

A soft whistle escapes him as he spots it. "There it is!" He's talking rapidly now. "I've read ancient Hebrew scriptures, which tell of this Ruler's star." Rising, he announces, "We must see him. We must go!"

Traversing the caravan routes of Persia, Babylon, and Syria for 1,200 miles, they ford broad rivers, pass ancient cities, cross barren deserts. For months they trek westward, day after day "following yonder star."

In Jerusalem they inquire, "Where is He that is born King of the Jews? For we have seen His star in the East and are come to worship Him." Worship? So the Babe is more than a king!

Now they follow the shining star till it rests over a simple Bethlehem stable. At early dawn neighbors gather to watch the richly robed travelers dismount. Joseph meets them at the door.

"We've come to see the Child, the King." The Wise Men fall before the Babe, faces to the floor—royal counselors doing homage, worshipping the Christ Child. Outside, their servants unload weighty chests from the camels and set gifts before the King. Heavy fragrances of frankincense and myrrh mingle to fill the room as one by one the boxes are opened.

A touch of the Boy-Child's tiny fingers, a final longing look, and the men rise to go. Camel bells soon fade in the brisk morning air.

We, too, travel at Christmas, visiting family and friends. Yet, like the Wise Men, the most important journey we make these hectic holidays is to draw nigh to Jesus Himself with the gift of our hearts.

© John Sloane

What Makes Christmas

Annie Johnson Flint

It was not the angels' singing
gave the Christmas thought,
not the precious gold and incense
by the Wise Men brought;

not the shining Star that led them
on their unknown way—
'twas the Christ within the manger
made the Christmas Day.

So 'tis not the tree and presents
make *our* Christmas Day;
'tis not what we get that counts,
but what we give away.

'Tis the joy of loving service
makes the glad hours bright,
thinking first of others' pleasure,
self put out of sight.

We need never mourn that Christmas
comes but once a year,
since the blessedness of giving
brings the Christmas cheer.

If we keep the Christmas spirit
in our hearts always,
through the whole year we can make it
Christmas every day.

Christmas Eve
Loretta Bauer Buckley

Holly wreath and mistletoe,
bayberry candle, drifting snow;
happiness and warmth and light,
boundless love this joyous night;
stockings hanging in a row,
eyes alight, hearts aglow;
softly spoken words of prayer,
dreams of starlight everywhere!

Light a Christmas Candle
Becky Jennings

Let's light a Christmas candle;
let's set the tree aglow;
let's trim the hearth with holly
and hang the mistletoe.

Let's send glad Yuletide greetings
to loved ones near and far;
let's scan the dark and velvet sky
for one bright, shining star.

Let's make some strings of popcorn
as they used to long ago;
let's listen for the sleigh bells
across the winter snow.

Let's gather by the fireside
with friends both old and new;
let's light a Christmas candle
to shine the whole year through.

Image © Visions/Gap PhotosLtd.

The Stillness of Christmas

John Peterson

The season of Christmas is usually associated with the hurry and thronging of crowds in the streets and shops. Sounds and songs fill the air; cheerful greetings, music and bustle, the chiming of bells—can there really be stillness at Christmas?

There must be. For stillness belongs in a special way to the deeper significance of the season. The writers of many of the best-loved Christmas hymns have called attention to that quietness, which is so essential a part of this festival time. The first stanza of Edmund Hamilton Sears' "It Came Upon a Midnight Clear" voices the thought of a world that in solemn stillness heard the angels sing.

The quietness of a night, under the open skies, rested on the shepherds as they watched their flocks; but a deeper, far deeper, stillness must have held them as the glory of the Lord shone round about them and fear gripped their hearts. And after the departure of the angels, after the glad tidings had been brought in word and melody, stillness—solemn and sacred—must have enveloped them.

This year, as never before, the children of men who would hear the song of the angels at Christmastime must first hear the Voice that says, "Be still, and know that I am God."

Bishop Brooks' famous hymn pictures a little town asleep in the quiet midnight hours: "O lit-tle town of Bethlehem, how still we see thee lie. Above thy deep and dreamless sleep the silent stars go by."

As the peaceful village sleeps through the silent night, the heavenly gift is given. There are no crowds or cheers. Humble shepherds hear the announcement and rejoice; but the little town sleeps on, in undisturbed repose: "How silently, how silently, the wondrous gift is given."

A silent Bethlehem, and within it a Mother and her Child, slumber in dreamless peace. Perhaps the most universally loved of all Christmas songs is the familiar "Silent Night!" How quiet, how still it must have been in that stable! "Silent night! Holy night! All is calm, all is bright round yon virgin Mother and Child. Holy Infant, so tender and mild, sleep in heavenly peace."

Into the Christian home there comes a certain stillness as the night before Christmas draws on. The excitement of preparation is over; the time to which all have looked forward for many weeks has come. Calm takes the place of feverish activity.

At such moments it may be that our thoughts turn to memories of Christmases of other years. The feeling comes that no matter how lovely Christmas may be this year, it can never again be so wonderful as it was during early childhood.

In these moments of stillness—as we look back to the days of long ago or rest from the bustle of Christmas preparation or consciously meditate on the meaning of Christmas—Christmas enters the heart. "No ear may hear His coming; but in this world of sin, where meek souls will receive Him still, the dear Christ enters in."

Where motherly love holds infant helplessness in close embrace, stillness is set to music, and we hear a lullaby. Every nation that celebrates the Nativity seems to have its own Christmas cradle song. How soft and low, how gently soothing, how much a part of Christmas these melodies are that lull earth's babes to rest!

Long after baby days have fled, we sing them. Along the trail of our remembered yesterdays, the star of reminiscence comes to rest above a shabby stable, fragrant with grasses, and there we find a lowly mother and her newborn Babe. Verily, it is Christmas again, and our hearts are at peace in the stillness.

True, there is a stillness at Christmas that may only be irksome to him who knows nothing of the glad tidings of great joy that make this a festival day to all who really do keep Christmas. But there is also a stillness of Christmas, a stillness that brings quietness to fearful, longing hearts, peace and unspeakable joy to those who receive the gift of our gracious God at Christmastime. "O dearest Jesus, Holy Child, make Thee a bed, soft, undefiled, within my heart, that it may be a quiet chamber kept for Thee."

Let there be music at Christmas. Let there be shouting and rejoicing. Let glad voices sing and greetings fill the air on this glad day. But let us learn also to know the stillness of Christmas, learn to love the Christmas silence.

How Beautiful
Eileen Spinelli

How beautiful, these wintry nights,
scented trees and twinkling lights,
ribboned gifts, stockings hung,
cookies baked and carols sung.

How beautiful, the love that blooms
in ragged hearts, familiar rooms.
Across a street or subway aisle—
how beautiful—a stranger's smile.

Christmas hath a beauty . . .
lovelier than the
world can show.
—Christina G. Rossetti

Christmas
Mary Louise Cheatham

We trim not only this year's tree
with silvered webs of memory,
but all the trees we ever had,
through happy Christmases, and sad.

Each ball suspended quivering bright
reflects a grown-up child's delight.
The clear glass bird that cannot sing
still hovers on a hopeful wing.

Along the gleaming ropes of beads
are strung old dreams, and loves, and needs.
Familiar angels hanging there
bring back a comfort and a prayer.

From starry tip to cotton snow
and worn, loved homemade creche below,
all Christmases that ever were
shine through the boughs of this year's fir!

Christmas Eve
Karen Elba

How very still it is tonight
in city and in town.
The little houses nestle close
like babes 'neath quilts of down.

The sky has sent an ermine wrap
for Mother Earth to wear
and placed a crown of diamond stars
upon her lovely hair.

All mankind waits the clarion call
across the frosty night;
even winds in leafless trees
have stopped their hurried flight.

One breathless moment, then the song
the herald angels sing—
bells rejoice, and Earth goes out
to meet her glorious King!

Hometown Christmas Eve
Doris A. Wise

We decorated every house;
we trimmed our every tree.
Our lawns we changed to Bethlehem
with scenes of the Nativity.

Tall candles glowed from porches,
broad eaves dripped gleaming lights,
and carol singers by the score
were heard on many nights.

On Christmas Eve we worshipped
with peace that candlelight imparts
and left the church at midnight
with decorated hearts!

A Christmas Carol

Edgar A. Guest

God bless you all this Christmas Day
and drive the cares and griefs away.
Oh, may the shining Bethlehem star,
which led the Wise Men from afar,
upon your heads, good sirs, still glow
to light the path that ye should go.

Within the walls may peace abide—
the peace for which the Savior died.
Though humble be the rafters here,

above them may the stars shine clear,
and in this home thou lovest well,
may excellence of spirit dwell.

God bless you all this Christmas Day.
May Bethlehem's star still light thy way
and guide thee to the perfect peace
when every fear and doubt shall cease.
And may thy home such glory know
as did the stable long ago.

ISBN-13: 978-0-8249-1348-9

Published by Ideals
An imprint of Worthy Publishing Group
A division of Worthy Media, Inc.
Nashville, Tennessee

Printed and bound in the U.S.A.
Printed on Weyerhauser Lynx. The paper used in this publication meets the minimum requirements of American National Standard for Information Sciences—Permanence of Paper for Printed Materials, ANSI Z39.48-1984.

Publisher, Peggy Schaefer
Editor, Melinda L. R. Rumbaugh
Permissions and Research, Kristi West
Copy Editor, Rachel Pate
Designer, Marisa Jackson

Cover: Image © Pat Tuson/Gap Photos Ltd.
Inside front cover: Image © Marcello Corti/Advocate Art
Inside back cover: Image © Marcello Corti/Advocate Art

Sheet music for "Jingle Bells" by Dick Torrans, Melode, Inc. Additional art credits: Art on pages 1, 28, 30–31, 34–35, and back cover by Kathy Rusynyk. The following pages contain art © [the artist]/Shutterstock.com: 2, Yudina Anna, il67; 4, Val_Iva, mexrix; 8, Seafowl; 11, Vector; 16–17, Magnia, Gross Maria; 19, liskus; 23, Sundra; 24, Erinphoto10; 27, MIGUEL GARCIA SAAVEDRA; 32–33, senina, Texturis, Ronnachai Palas, Wisut, Mark Carrel; 36, TomZa, lenavdovinaart; 38–39, Baleika Tamara, taniasneg; 40–41, alex.makarova; 42, Vector, wacomka; 44–49, Naticka; 51, Radiocat, Dobrynina Elena; 52–53, Innakote, Kozyrina Olga; 54, Dobrynina Elena; 58–59, Marina Grau, happykanppy; 60, Ozerina Anna, Curly Pat; 64, Dobrynina Elena.

ACKNOWLEDGMENTS:

WILSON, RALPH F. "Christmas Travelers" Copyright © Ralph F. Wilson, www.joyfulheart.com. All rights reserved. Used by permission.

OUR THANKS to the following authors or their heirs: Beverly J. Anderson, June Master Bacher, Winnie Barnett, Deborah A. Bennett, Rowena Bastin Bennett, Elveira Blust, Nora M. Bozeman, Anne Kennedy Brady, Loretta Bauer Buckley, Gail Brook Burket, Eileen Burnett, Mary Louise Cheatham, Thomas Curtis Clark, Lucille Crumley, Joseph F. Daniel, George L. Ehrman, G. Farfan, Harriet Feltham, Loise Pinkerton Fritz, Gracia Grindal, Edgar A. Guest, Nelle Hardgrove, Becky Jennings, Pamela Kennedy, Faith E. Kessi, Jean E. Koch, Robert D. Little, Pamela Love, Dona Maxey, Virginia Midgett, Solveig Paulson Russell, Diane Skinner, Eileen Spinelli, W.L. Stidger, Nancy Byrd Turner, Harriet Whipple, Marjorie Wilson, Elisabeth Weaver Winstead, Doris A. Wise. Scripture quotations are taken from King James Version (KJV).

Every effort has been made to establish ownership and use of each selection in this book. If contacted, the publisher will be pleased to rectify any inadvertent errors or omissions in subsequent editions.

Join the community of *Ideals* readers on Facebook at: www.facebook.com/IdealsMagazine
Readers are invited to submit original poetry and prose for possible use in future publications. Please send no more than four typed submissions to: *Ideals* submissions, Worthy Publishing Group, 6100 Tower Circle, Suite 210, Franklin, Tennessee 37067. Manuscripts will be returned if a self-addressed stamped envelope is included.